# An Introduction to Heat Pumps

# An Introduction To Heat Pumps

## John A. Sumner

Prism Press

First Published in Great Britain 1976 by

PRISM PRESS
Stable Court
Chalmington
Dorchester
Dorset DT2 0HB

Second Edition published 1980

Copyright John Sumner 1976
Copyright John Sumner's Estate 1980

ISBN 0  907061 00 1

Printed and Bound in Great Britain
by Purnell and Sons (Book Production) Ltd.,
Paulton, Bristol

# Contents

# Introduction

In January 1975 The Times published a letter in which I described the operation of my heat pump. I installed it in my house in 1960 and since then it has been in continuous use and has provided enormous savings in fuel and money. My letter provoked a sackful of enquiries. What is a heat pump? How does it work? What does it save in fuel and money? Where can I get one? This book aims to answer all of these questions concisely. No attempt has been made herein to deal with design details or advanced theory. These are contained in my published book *'Domestic Heat Pumps'*, and the forthcoming *'Practical Heat Pumps'*.

This book will generally confine itself to what one can expect from a heat pump installation. At present there is very little research work being done although there are signs that the Government is finally awakening from its long slumber. Nevertheless nowhere in the world today can one buy an efficient, reliable, rigorously designed domestic heat pump. In this book I shall endeavour to present a minimum specification as well as general principles to be followed if your heat pump is to succeed.

A heat pump is a very simple machine consisting of three main components. My first domestic unit utilised two motor car radiators (forming the evaporator and condenser of Fig. 2) and a Villiers motor cycle engine (with adapted valve sequence) driven by an electric motor. A small redundant auto engine and radiator works producing say, 10,000 units a year could with very little adaptation produce even more heat pumps. One such converted engine could save twice as much fuel as was wasted by the automobile engine.

There is nothing mysterious about a heat pump. Many readers will already possess one in the form of a refrigerator or deep freeze, which extracts heat from food at around freezing point and expels this heat at a higher temperature through a duct into the kitchen or wherever. Contrary to popular opinion a heat pump is a refrigerator and not a 'reversed refrigerator'. One purpose of this book is to emphasize two major points which relate to the provision of heat in order to maintain a domestic dwelling at 70°F (21°C). Firstly, when such heat is derived from the combustion of fuel there is a gradual fall from a high to a lower temperature. When such heat is provided by a heat pump the process commences at a lower temperature and is 'pumped up' to the required higher temperature. Secondly, given an efficiently driven heat pump with an efficiency ratio (heat given out : heat as work put in) of three to one, the fuel consumed to provide the given amount of heat is less than will be used by any other practical method of providing that heat. Such a machine can return 100 per cent of the heat available in the fuel used to drive it and, in certain cases, more than 100 per cent.

Unfortunately, there is no accurate scientific term in use to describe the ratio of Heat Output : Work Expended in relation to the operation of a heat pump. In this book the term 'Co-efficient of Heating' or C.H. is used in contra-distinction to the term 'Co-efficient of Cooling' to describe the ratio Heat Extracted : Work Expended relating to a refrigerator.

# What is a Heat Pump?

A heat pump is **not** a 'reversed refrigerator'. It **is** a refrigerator which has the same components and does exactly the same basic things as the domestic refrigerator in your kitchen. A refrigerator's function is to remove heat from some space whereas the function of a heat pump is to deliver heat to a room. The domestic refrigerator is arranged so that air is passed over a vessel, called an *evaporator*, which is connected to the suction side of a *compressor* (see Fig. 2) and which contains a liquid of the type used and supplied under pressure in the small cylinders used to re-fill cigarette lighters. When the pressure on this liquid is reduced, as happens when it is fed into the lighter or as the *compressor* draws vapour from the *evaporator*, the liquid 'boils' and changes into a vapour. This change of state demands heat — which is why your cigarette lighter becomes very cold when you re-fill it. In this manner heat is taken from the air passing over the *evaporator* so that the air falls in temperature and is returned (several times) to the food space in your refrigerator as cold air.

Now, from a refrigeration standpoint, a difficulty arises. The compressor has taken the cooled suction gas and compressed it, thereby raising the temperature from, say, 0°C to 50°C. As the gas has now to be returned to the *evaporator* it is necessary to extract heat and restore the low temperature. We can now consider the function of the heat pump. The hot compressed gas can now be led into the *condenser* where air or water can be arranged in a manner to abstract the heat. In the domestic refrigerator this abstracted heat can be dissipated into the kitchen; in the heat pump the high temperature heat can be used to fulfil the purpose of heating a room.

The cycle of operations is now nearly complete. The cooled, but still warm, gas has now condensed into a liquid and is allowed to pass through a restriction called an *expansion valve* which reduced pressure and allows the return to the *evaporator*, where the cycle recommences. The *compressor* of a heat pump is very similar in size, construction and operation to an 850 c.c. motor car engine, when air is used as the cooling and heating medium. The *evaporator* and *condenser* are equivalent in size to the radiator and internal heater of the motor car and serve similar purposes.

# Why Should I Use a Heat Pump?

The short answer is that you require heat which, in the cold winter months will be at a temperature higher than that of the ambient air surrounding the room and sometimes, in summer, will be required at a lower relative temperature. The first requirement is most easily met by striking a match to cause coal or oil to be burned by a chemical process which produces heat at about 600°C. The heat thus made available must then be permitted to fall to a temperature around 70°F (21°C) to heat the room. As it continues to fall in temperature the heat will escape from the room and will be absorbed by the earth, air and water surrounding us at about 0°C.

Nature imposes penalties in the processes of creation and usage of heat. Firstly, the 1 lb of coal or oil from which the heat was derived, which took many millions of years to make, has disappeared in a matter of minutes leaving that much less for the future. Secondly, she decrees that we can never obtain, even in the most efficient circumstances, more than about 80 per cent of the heat potential in the fuel. For most domestic combustion processes we obtain about 50 per cent of this potential heat. The remainder escapes via the chimney and as unconsumed fuel to our ambient surroundings. So, as an average, in order to obtain the heat at 21°C available in 1 lb of fuel by direct combustion, 2 lbs of fuel must be destroyed and the total heat from these 2 lbs will ultimately be absorbed by our ambient surroundings.

It is fortunate that we live on this earth in what could be called a bath or blanket of ambient heat varying in temperature from about 0°C to about 22°C in Britain. All the heat generated by combustion ultimately sinks into this cushion and if it did not exist this heat would continue to fall in temperature until it reached absolute zero (-273°C) at which the heat would be completely void of both temperature and energy.

It is the presence of this surrounding cushion of *useful* heat that makes the operation of the heat pump possible. The reader will, at first, question whether heat at or near freezing point temperature can properly be classified as 'heat'. This is because experience has led us to use an artificial scale to determine heat energy in which the sense of touch uses blood or body temperatures of 34.4°C as the touchstone. Water freezes at 0°C and turns into steam at 100°C and these limiting changes of state tend to indicate our limit of 'coldness' as being 0°C, or freezing point. In fact, a body is only 'cold', i.e. has no energy or temperature, when it is 273°C or 496°F below freezing point. Scientifically, and practically, when considering heat pumps it is necessary to use a different, or 'absolute' scale of temperature. This is shown in °K instead of °C and has equivalent values as follows:

0°K = -273°C = absolute zero
273°K = 0°C = freezing point of water
373°K = 100°C = boiling point of water
(i.e. °K = °C + 273°)

In what follows we must consider 'temperature' as a measure of 'heat energy'. A given quantity of a substance at freezing point temperature must be considered as having 273 units of heat energy, i.e. as being 273°K 'hot' and at boiling point as having 373 units of heat energy, and so on.

Figure 1 shows a scientifically inaccurate but practical way of obtaining heat at 21°C, i.e. 294°K, by two different methods. The heat energy in a given parcel of fuel is assumed to be proportional to the height of the fuel above the bottom of the pit which is 273 feet below ground level. A parcel of fuel at the top of the building 315 feet high (or 588 feet above the pit) will therefore contain 588 energy units. If this parcel is allowed to fall on to a platform 21 feet above ground level, i.e. at 21°C or 294°K, 294 units will be dissipated and only 294 energy units become available. This process of falling (representing direct combustion at 50 per cent efficiency) results in an energy loss of 294 units.

With the heat pump we first take a parcel of fuel, possessing 273 energy units, from the huge store lying at ground level (at 0°C or 273°K) and do compression work representing 21 units of energy so as to lift the parcel 21 feet to platform height so that it contains 273 + 21 or 294 energy units. In the direct combustion case we lose 294 units of energy

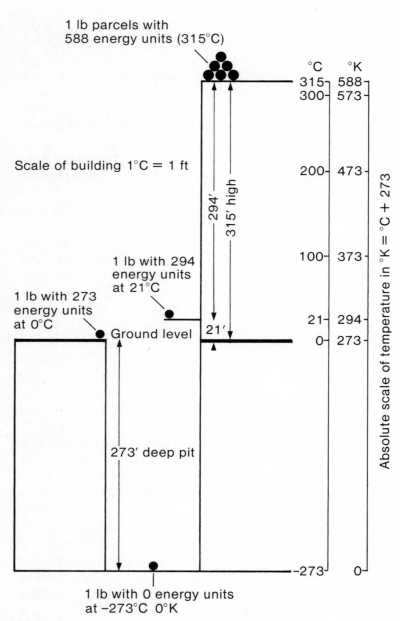

1 lb parcels with
588 energy units (315°C)

°C    °K

315  588
300  573

Scale of building 1°C = 1 ft

200  473

Absolute scale of temperature in °K = °C + 273

294'    315' high

100  373

1 lb with 294
energy units
at 21°C

1 lb with 273
energy units
at 0°C

21  294
Ground level    21'    0  273

273' deep pit

-273  0

1 lb with 0 energy units
at −273°C  0°K

**Figure 1.**

14

and in the second case we lose only 21 units in compression work to achieve the desired 294 final energy units. In this case the 'ideal' heat pump process is 294 ÷ 21 or 14 times as efficient as the direct burning process. It will be noted that any increase in the height above ground to which the heat pump must lift the parcel, i.e. any increase in the temperature differences between which the heat pump will work, will reduce this advantage of 14. If this height is increased from 21°C to 42°C (315°K) then it would require 42 work units and our advantage of 14 falls to 294 ÷ 42 = 7. The discerning reader will have noted that we are considering a ratio of Heat Output : Work Done and, if the ratio is considered in terms of temperature (with $t_1$ representing the upper and $t_2$ the lower temperature) then:

$$\frac{\text{Heat Output}}{\text{Work Done}} = \frac{t_1}{t_1 - t_2} = \frac{294}{294 - 273} = 14$$

The difference between the direct combustion process and the heat pump process will now be evident. The direct combustion process is one of *subtraction* in which we subtract and waste 294 units from fuel which contains, say, 588 units (at 588°K or 315°C) to obtain 294 useful units. By comparison the heat pump process is one of *addition* in that we commence with a quantity of air or water already containing 273 units and then add to it by some means 21 units only, to obtain the required quantity of 294 units.

We are therefore led to pose these two questions:

a)    Is there a less wasteful method of producing heat at a temperature of 294°K or 21°C than by the direct burning of fuel?

b) Can we find a method of adding heat to the substantial existing quantity of heat at 273°K or more which is contained in our ambient surroundings and thereby raise the temperature of the whole parcel to 294°K?

There is in fact such a method available in the heat pump.

The original types of heat pumps were based upon the compression and expansion of air. Subsequently it was found that it was more convenient to transfer the ambient heat at 0°C to a volatile liquid (similar to that used in cigarette lighters) which boils at 0°C. The resulting vapour could then be compressed to 21°C, or such higher temperature as was required. Details of these methods are given in my more comprehensive book *Domestic Heat Pumps* and are shown here in diagrammatic form in Figs. 2 and 3. At this stage, therefore, it must be accepted that in an ideal heat pump process we are able to take a parcel of ambient heat which already contains 273 energy units, and by compression, represented by a further 21 units of energy, raise the temperature of the air or vapour to the required 294 units. But, unfortunately, to obtain the power required we must expend 2.5 units to provide each unit of power, which means that 53 units, not 21, must be added in order to reach the required 294 units.

It is evident that the heat pump, in expending only 33 units to provide 294 units, represents a useful fuel saving device when it is compared with more conventional methods of heating where, by direct combustion, 294 of the original 588 units are wasted (see Fig. 1).

Let us translate these somewhat abstract ideas into everyday practical values. 11 lbs (5kg) of oil has a potential heat value of about 2 Therms (200,000 Btu, 211 MJ, or 59 kW/h). On an average, one half of this potential heat (5.5 lbs) is lost in the normal small oil-fired boiler so 1 therm of heat at 21°C, or the equivalent of only 5.5 lbs of oil, becomes available for heating your house. Half of the oil burnt is wasted.

Now consider the fuel consumption if a heat pump is used. First, in order to maintain a room at a temperature of 21°C, the heat source, whether it be radiators, the floor, warm air, etc. must be at a higher temperature, say at 42°C. So, in practice, we must now provide 422 heat units to maintain the room at 21°C (294°K). Now our ratio of Heat Output : Work Done becomes $294 \div 42 = 7$. Further, for each unit of power put in as compression work only about 60 per cent will be available as useful work within the cycle. This further reduces our ration to $294 \div 56 = 5.25$. Therefore the reciprocal of the ratio is $1 \div 5.25 = 0.19$.

We can now work out the oil consumption to obtain 1 therm of heat (equivalent to 5.5 lbs of oil) if the practical heat pump described above is used:

$$\frac{\text{Heat Output}}{\text{Power Input}} = \frac{1}{0.19} = \frac{1 \text{ therm}}{0.19 \text{ therm}} = \frac{\text{Heat in 5.5 lbs of oil}}{\text{Heat in 1.05 lbs of oil}}$$

So, when we had to burn 11 lbs of oil with direct combustion to obtain 1 therm of heat, the heat pump power input fuel requirement is equivalent only to the heat from 1.05 lbs of oil so far.

But the picture is not yet complete. We must have a driving agent to rotate the compressor and provide the power and to do this we must burn more fuel. This means that if the driving agent operates at an average efficiency of 33 per cent we shall have to burn 3 x 1.05 lbs of oil to obtain 1 therm of heat as opposed to the 11 lbs if an oil burner is used at 50 per cent efficiency.

If the heat pump is driven by an electric motor fed from a modern power station you should receive 33 per cent of the heat in the fuel as the electric power heat equivalent. If, therefore, you use electricity in a cooker or radiator, you would obtain, as heat, 33 per cent of the heat in the fuel burned at the power station. If however, you use the same amount of electricity to drive the heat pump electric motor described above you would obtain 5.25 times as much heat as would be given by the electric radiator; it is shown later that a practical heat pump gives an actual factor of 3, instead of 5.25.

It is a more economic proposition to use an oil engine to drive the compressor of the heat pump. The quantity of heat from the heat pump to the house will be the same in both cases but with the oil engine consuming 3.15 lbs of oil for each therm of heat output, of which 1.05 lbs is used as power, leaving us with the heat from 2.1 lbs of oil which can be utilised for house heating.

The question as to why you should use a heat pump has, therefore, two answers:
a)    If you use a heat pump to obtain a given

amount of heat at 21°C you will use approximately one third to one quarter of the fuel that would be used by direct combustion. This also, of course, extends by three or four times the life of that fuel's reserves.

b)  By using only one third to one quarter of the fuel to achieve the same result, logically you can be saving two-thirds to three-quarters of your fuel bills.

In practice, a heat pump would have to work at a higher temperature than 21°C in order to maintain a house at that temperature. So let us take a practical example of the economy achieved by a heat pump which has been operating between 0°C and 60°C (273 and 333°K) for 15 years to maintain my house of 1500 sq ft at 21°C. The heat delivered to the house by the heat pump was at the rate of 12.4 kW/h and, during each heating season has averaged 1230 therms or 37,000 kW/h, into hot water at 130°F (55°C). The heat pump is driven by an electric motor consuming 4.2kW/h with a total consumption per heating season of 12016 kW/h. The practical answers to (a) and (b) above for this specific case are therefore:

a)  One third of the fuel that would be used by direct combustion is used by the heat pump driven by an electric motor to provide 1230 therms.

b)  1230 therms of heat can be provided to a house with annual heat consumption and costs (1980) as shown below in Table 1.

This table gives practical answers to the question posed earlier, proved in practice in my own house, so far as the electric motor driven heat pump is concerned. As time proceeds and as present crude heat pump design improves, coupled with continual increases in fuel prices, the costs savings shown above will be enhanced proportionally. The relatively few heat pumps at present in use in the Western world, now relatively expensive because of low demand, could be replaced by cheaper mass-produced machines available from the growing pool of redundant machinery and labour languishing in the gradually declining motor car industry.

**Table 1**
**Cost of providing 1230 therms of heat to a house**
(November 1979)

| Heat Source | Heat Purchased | Fuel Purchased | Cost 1976 | 1980 |
|---|---|---|---|---|
| Oil Burner | 2460 therms | 1367 gallons | 312 | 751 |
| Heat Pump with C.H. = 3 | 410 therms | 12016 kW/h | 106 | 362 |

# What is the "Efficiency" of a Heat Pump?

It is measured in the same way that you measure the 'efficiency' of your car, except that you substitute heat values for miles and gallons.

To measure car efficiency you would put in one gallon (say G gallons) of petrol and then run the car, noting the miles run (say M miles) until the petrol was exhausted. If the mileage run was 20 miles the ratio of miles to the gallon is 20 to 1 or 20 m.p.g. But, if you measure the ratio of 'Useful heat available' to 'Heat available in fuel used' an entirely different picture emerges. Engineers denote this ration by the symbol $\epsilon$ which must always have a value less than unity. The approximate value of $\epsilon$ for direct combustion is as follows:

**Table 2**

| | Heat Generator | | | |
| Value of | Modern Power station | Car engine | Oil burner | Gas burner |
| --- | --- | --- | --- | --- |
| Heat in fuel lost | 62% | 75% | 50% | 40% |
| Useful heat available $\epsilon$ | 38% | 25% | 50% | 60% |
| Original heat in fuel | 100% | 100% | 100% | 100% |

In Fig. 1 the much more efficient alternative method of obtaining 'Useful Heat' by means of a heat pump was shown. It was shown that approximately 67 per cent of the required heat was collected from the environment at about 273°K (0°C) and was then pumped up to a useful higher temperature of about 294°K (21°C), finally providing us with an amount of heat = 0.67 + 0.33 = 1.0 or equal to the original heat in the fuel.

Now, to have found a method of gainfully using all of the heat available in the fuel consumed is an important achievement. We shall therefore obtain from the heat pump (per unit of fuel consumed) three times as much heat as an electric fire can give, twice as much heat as an oil burner can give and more than one and a half times that from a gas burner.

**Table 3**
**Fuel required to provide one unit of heat into a room using various methods of heating**

| Heating method | Heat to room (a) | Fuel used per unit into room (b) | Ratio a/b |
|---|---|---|---|
| Electricity | 1 | 3 | 0.33 |
| Oil burner | 1 | 2 | 0.5 |
| Gas burner | 1 | 1.7 | 0.6 |
| Heat pump, electric drive | 1 | 1 | 1 |
| Heat pump, oil engine | 1 | 0.71 | 1.4 |

In practice, the heat pump can provide even more than 100 per cent of the heat which was initially available in the fuel used. If, for example, we drive a heat pump by an oil engine (which wastes to atmosphere 67 per cent of the heat in the oil consumed) it is possible to recover, as useful heat, at least 60 per cent of the 67 per cent waste heat, i.e. 40 per cent of the total available heat in the fuel. Thus we have as 'available heat' — 0.67 + 0.33 (as before) + 0.4 = 1.4. In other words almost one and a half times as much heat as was available in the fuel consumed. This gives us a ratio of 'heat available' to 'heat originally in the fuel' of 140% to 100% or 1.4:1.

Two somewhat imprecise definitions of preferred heat pump efficiency have now been formulated.

1.  The amount of heat given to the room shall be equal to, or greater than, the heat which was in the fuel consumed in driving the heat pump.
2.  In those cases where the power input to the heat pump has a value of $\epsilon = 0.33$, the ratio of Heat Output to Heat Input shall have a minimum value of 3 (this being the reciprocal value of $\epsilon = 0.33$).

The supplier of an efficient domestic heat pump should guarantee a constant return of three times as much heat as is put in to drive the machine.

# What Types of Heat Pump Are Available?

A broad classification of the various types of heat pump can be made as follows:

**Air-to-Air**

Ambient air varying widely in temperature from time to time is used as the source of low-grade heat supplying heat to the evaporator. A separate supply of ambient air, probably mixed with warmer re-circulated air is then heated by passing through a condenser.

**'Constempair' Air-to Air**

Arrangements are made, without recourse to external energy sources, to provide ambient air at a constant temperature of the order of 46°F (8°C) to the heat pump evaporator. A separate supply of ambient air, as for type 1, is then provided to be heated at the condenser.

**Air-to-Water**

Ambient air is the source of low-grade heat and the condenser supplies heat to a circulated hot-water system.

**Water-to-Air**

In this case low-grade heat is supplied to the evaporator from a body of water or from an anti-freeze liquid circulating through pipes buried in the earth or water. Alternatively a liquid may circulate through solar cells and so be heated before entering the evaporator. Heat from the condenser is then abstracted by circulated air.

**Water-to-Water**

This arrangement uses the evaporator as in the water-to-air with a condenser as in the air-to-water.

**Air-to-Air**

The advantage of this type lies in the ease and apparent cheapness of this method of collecting low-grade heat. As will be seen from Fig. 2 ambient air is blown (or drawn) through the evaporator by means of a fan. There are, however, serious disadvantages which occur when using this method. These are as follows:

a)  It is not possible to move air without generating some noise, however small the noise intensity. Unless the parameters of the fan are carefully chosen a complication of noise and wasted fan power can occur.

b)  A most serious disadvantage is due to the fact that, when the ambient air temperature falls, the demand for heat from the condenser increases simultaneously with a falling away of heat at the evaporator. The net effect is a fall in the temperature and pressure in both evaporator and condenser, and therefore in the output of the machine.

c)  In any type of heat pump the chief requirement, in order to give high efficiency and long compressor life, is to keep the compressor suction temperature (which is closely linked with suction pressure) as constant as possible. If we assume a variation in ambient air temperature between -3°C and 12°C, when using Freon 12 ($CCl_2F_2$) as the refrigerant, the following variations in suction gas pressure and volume occur and such variations in ambient air temperatures can occur in one day.

| Temp. | Gas Pressure p.s.i.a. | Volume $ft^3/lbs$ | Average % Pressure | Variation in Volume |
|---|---|---|---|---|
| -3°C | 41 | 1.00 | | |
| 0°C | 45 | 0.877 | 1.6 p.s.i.a. | 0.03 $ft^3$ per |
| 8°C | 56 | 0.725 | per 1°C | 1 p.s.i.a. |
| 12°C | 65 | 0.53 | | |

The amount of heat taken in by the compressor is proportional to the volume of refrigerant vapour taken in at each stroke and the heat output and driving motor demand increases or decreases in proportion to that volume. It is obvious that this feature compels a compromise in design and/or a risk of failure in the compressor unit, sometimes within a year.

Recently, the American Electric Power Service Corporation published an analysis of service record failures on air-to-air pumps. The analysis gave the following data:

| | | |
|---|---|---|
| 1968—73 | Maintenance and servicing costs due to compressor failure | 28 per cent |
| 1968—73 | Fan motor failures | 15 per cent |
| 1965—73 | Warranty compressor failure rates % per unit year | 10 per cent |

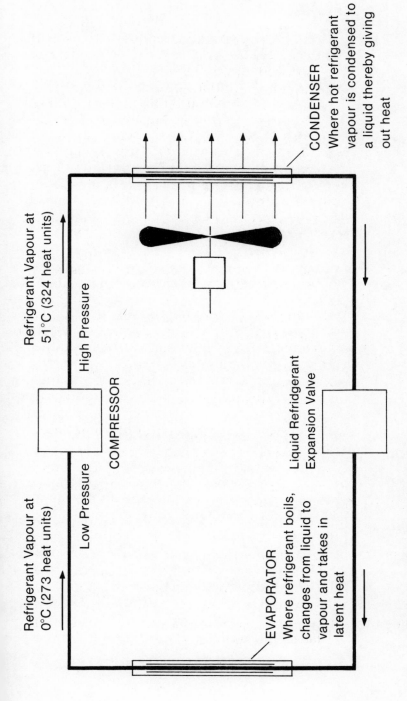

Figure 2. Air-toAir heat pump

Refrigerant Vapour at 51°C (324 heat units)

High Pressure

CONDENSER
Where hot refrigerant vapour is condensed to a liquid thereby giving out heat

COMPRESSOR

Refrigerant Vapour at 0°C (273 heat units)

Low Pressure

Liquid Refridgerant Expansion Valve

EVAPORATOR
Where refrigerant boils, changes from liquid to vapour and takes in latent heat

There is no reason to suppose that should a similar analysis be carried out today it would produce much improved data.

Probably the most serious hazard of the ordinary air-to-air heat pump is the problem of frost or ice formation on the evaporator surfaces. At an incoming ambient air temperature below about 10°C water held in the air separates out as the temperature falls across the evaporator and forms ice on its surface. When the air enters at a lower temperature around 0°C, with lower humidity, frost forms on the evaporator surfaces. Both ice and frost reduce heat intake to the evaporator and also restrict the passage of air. The methods adopted to try and prevent ice and frost formation add to the inefficiency of the heat pump. One method of de-icing is to reverse the flow of refrigerant so that hot refrigerant flows through the evaporator instead of through the condenser; as a result the house ceases to be heated. Another method is to install electric heating elements on the evaporator to melt the ice. This means that heat representing one-third of the heat in the fuel consumed is given, as electricity, to a machine that is producing, at times, much less than three times as much heat as is used to drive it. Monitored tests taken during 1972/74 by Mr E.G.A. Goodall suggest that over an average winter an air type heat pump would probably give a value of C.H. = 2 which does not comply with the value of C.H. = 3 specified in this book as a minimum value which would justify the use of a heat pump.

One advantage of the air-to-air heat pump

is its ability to provide cold air to the house as well as hot air. By providing a reversing valve plus four special non-return valves and an additional thermal expansion valve the flow of the refrigerant can be reversed so that the condenser which normally heats the air entering the house acts as an evaporator which cools this air. Compressor and coil sizes must be carefully chosen to allow heat entering the normal evaporator coil to escape freely. Failure to permit free escape can cause high working temperatures and pressures; thus giving severe compressor overloading.

**Air-to-Air (at constant suction pressure)**

This patented type of heat pump, recently introduced as the 'Constempair' heat pump, claims to have overcome the serious disadvantages of air-to-air heat pumps. It also has the advantages, first, of eliminating supplementary electric resistance heating of the evaporator when operating in the heating mode. It is claimed that suction pressure and temperature and also compressor loading does not vary more than five per cent between ambient air temperatures from -5°C to 15°C. Also, it claims to have eliminated the need for the four non-return valves and the extra thermal expansion valve. This type of heat pump can be changed from the heating to the cooling mode by a reversal of the air flow direction only and without using reversing or one-way valves etc.

If these claims are substantiated, the effect will be to transform the air type evaporator and the use of ambient air from an uncertain and inefficient status to the cheapest and most efficient component and low-grade heat source, certainly for ambient air temperature conditions in Britain.

## Air-to-Water

This type uses ambient air as the low-grade heat source. The condenser consists of a cylindrical two-circuit heat exchanger with the refrigerant entering the cylinder at one end and hot circulating water from the house entering the second circuit in counterflow. This type suffers all the disadvantages of widely varying refrigerant pressure and volume, and ice and frost troubles, as referred to in the air-to-air machine.

## Type 3 and Type 4

These two types, water-to-air and water-to-water, are put together here because of their common characteristic of using water (or anti-freeze solution) as the medium which collects and circulates the incoming low-grade heat. The low-grade heat collecting system may be one of several types:

a) A coil of pipes laid in soil to collect solar heat stored in the earth (see page 39).

b) A coil of plastic hose laid on the soil surface to collect solar heat directly in the daytime and heat from ambient air during darkness.

c) Solar panels.

d) A coil of pipes laid directly in a large body of water.

e) Water from a well or borehole.

The buried pipe coil system is the most efficient since it will provide heat throughout the heating season that permits both suction gas pressure and volume to remain constant to within about 1 per cent. It is relatively

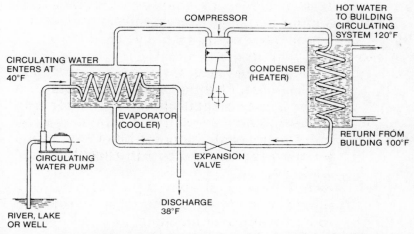

**Figure 3. Heat Pump installation using water as source of low grade heat.**

cheap to install, the total cost being not greater than the cost of replacing a compressor or driving motor which is liable to fail in a relatively short time if subjected to widely varying loads and pressures. The minimum superficial ground area required is of the order of 12 square yards. It is preferable to use water mixed with anti-freeze liquid as the incoming temperature of the circulating medium remains constant at about 0°C.

An alternative to the use of an anti-freeze solution as the circulating medium in the pipe system is to insert the actual refrigerant into the buried coil so that the coil becomes the heat pump evaporator. This permits of increased efficiency since it avoids the need for a circulating pump and the temperature drop in the secondary circuit. Unfortunately, like so many other phases of heat pump development, there is little experience available as to the possibilities of vapour locks or oil loss.

In a few instances a body of moving water, a well or borehole might be available. In the case of moving water it is quite possible to use refrigerant directly into a coil approximately 30 to 40 metres in length. With wells or boreholes a secondary circuit should be used in order to prevent blockage of the evaporator passages by particles of chalk or grit.

# How Should I Choose a Heat Pump?

First you should know what a practical heat pump consists of. It is a fairly simple machine and is exactly the same as your domestic refrigerator or deep-freeze except that the component parts are somewhat larger and will occupy a space about twice as large as a domestic refrigerator. The heat pump must have the following minimum number of components:

a)  A high temperature heat exchanger (the condenser).

b)  A low temperature heat exchanger (the evaporator).

c)  A sub-cooling heat exchanger.

d)  A compressor.

e)  An expansion or metering valve.

f)  An engine or electric motor for driving the compressor.

The first four components are very similar in function and capacity to the engine, two radiators and carburettor of an 850 c.c. motor car engine. The components would be connected together by pipes conveying the refrigerant in the manner described in Figs. 2 and 3.

## Size of House and Maximum Heat Requirements

Measure the floor area and room height of each room to be heated which, if added together, will give a total cubic capacity for the house. The next step is to find the heat loss through the walls, ceilings and floor when the inside space is at a pre-determined temperature, say 68°F (20°C) and the outside ambient air is at 32°F (0°C); this will depend upon the value of insulation provided. As a rough rule it may be assumed that a well insulated house will lose 3.5 Btu/h (say 1W) per cubic foot of space.

The figures given in the table below should be used with caution and as representing a reasonably high standard of insulation throughout the house. They are based on a room temperature of 68°F (20°C) with an outdoor ambient temperature of 32°F (0°C); it should be noted that these figures represent maximum demands which occur for ony about 5 per cent of the heating season. Average demand over the season will be about 65 per cent of the demands shown in the table, except for low-grade heat requirements.

**Table 4**

| Cubic Capacity of Dwelling | Max demand for heat | | Max demand of heat C.H. = 3 | | Low grade heat reqd | |
|---|---|---|---|---|---|---|
| cub. ft. | Btu | kW | Btu | kW | Btu | kW |
| 8,000 | 30,000 | 9.0 | 10,000 | 3.0 | 20,000 | 6.0 |
| 12,000 | 40,000 | 12.5 | 13,500 | 4.1 | 26,500 | 8.2 |
| 16,000 | 60,000 | 16.5 | 20,000 | 6.0 | 40,000 | 12.0 |

This may give values obtained as follows:
Btu/h = $q_1$ at 60°C.

a) Heat required to house                45,000 Btu/hr = at 60°C
b) Work put in to drive the machine    15,000 Btu/hr = 4.4kW
c) Balance required from ambient air   30,000 Btu/hr = $q_2$ at 0°C
    or water etc.

The reader can now translate the above hourly requirements into the seasonal requirements shown earlier in Table 1, having in mind that 1 therm of heat = 100,000 Btu of heat. If his heat pump ran at full load for 2730 hours during the heating season, the amount of heat supplied to the house would be 2730 x 45,000 Btu which is equal to 1230 therms.

The total power for which he pays would be 2730 hours x 4.4 kW or 12,012 kWh (electrical units).

The reader will now, it is hoped, see more clearly the options (shown in Table 1) which are open to him in order to obtain 1230 therms of heat during the heating season.

First he can purchase and burn 13,600 lbs (1360 gallons) of oil (with a calorific value of 18,000 Btu per lb) for £751 and burn it at 50 per cent efficiency.

Second he can purchase 1230 therms divided by 3412 or 36,036 electrical units (kWh) at, say, 3.01p per kWh for £1063 and use electric radiators or storage heaters.

Third he can gather from ambient earth, air or water 67 per cent of his seasonal heat requirements at 0°C, i.e. 820 therms, then obtain an electrically driven heat pump that will consume 12,018 kWh (410 therms) at 3.01p and will produce at 60°C the 1230

therms of heat that he requires at a cost of
£362.

# How Can I Obtain Ambient (Low-grade) Heat?

This aspect has been considered briefly at an earlier stage in the book but will now be re-considered in rather more detail.

**Air as the Source of Low-Grade Heat**

Ambient air, at first sight, would appear to be the most suitable form of low-grade heat. It is abundant in quantity and requires no apparatus or components to collect it, except for a fan to provide movement through the heat pump evaporator. But, in fact, the use of untreated air as a heat source presents very serious problems that were enumerated earlier. In my view the current type of heat pump using untreated air as the low-grade heat source, in Britain, will result in efficiencies which are so low, and associated difficulties in operation which are so great, as to discredit the normal air evaporator type heat pump as a successful fuel saver. If, however, it becomes possible to treat air so as to eliminate icing problems and maintain a constant evaporator pressure it is likely that air may still be used as the source of low-grade heat.

## Water as the Source of Low-Grade Heat

To obtain some measure of this requirement, consider a swimming pool with a volume of 2100 cu ft and containing 13,500 gallons of water. To meet the low-grade heat requirement of 30,000 Btu/h would reduce the water temperature by 1°C each 8 hours. Assuming that the water was initially at 7°C it would be reduced to a safe minimum of 2°C in 40 hours of operation of the heat pump. Experience shows, however, that relatively short periods of very cold weather might necessitate running the heat pump continuously for one or two periods of 48 hours. This clearly shows that a swimming pool capacity is inadequate. By comparison, a well or stream of water 5 feet wide by 6 feet deep moving at a rate of 65 feet per hour would provide the necessary low-grade heat at practically constant temperature.

## Solar Heat as the Source of Low-Grade Heat

Apart from treated air or water from streams or wells, solar heat is the best source of low-grade heat. Unfortunately many unjustified claims are being made for solar heat collectors which these notes may help to dispel. First there is the type of collector which takes in heat during daylight hours. Peak rates of collection may approach 1 $kW/h/m^2$ of collector but the average daily collection rate in winter is likely to be of the order of 0.03 kW/h or, say, 100 $Btu/h/m^2$. For an installation of the size being considered here, direct collection without storage facilities would involve considerable expense for the 300 $m^2$ of collector required. The collecting fluid would need to be an anti-freeze medium and the heat pump would suffer from the disadvantage of relatively high evaporator temperatures during daylight hours and unduly low temperatures at night, unless large and expensive flow water storage was installed.

## Soil as the Source of Low-Grade Heat

The most suitable form of solar heat to use with a heat pump is solar heat stored in the earth. It is strange that the use of this immense source of heat is so often decried. It is held that the average house plot does not contain sufficient land for the necessary buried pipes. Yet only 12 sq yds is required, as a minimum, and the land remains available for normal use as a lawn or whatever. It is also held that the cost of installation is too high, but, since the ground coil heat pump ensures a value of C.H. = 3 compared with a value of C.H. = 2 when using ambient air, there is an annual saving of one-third in electricity consumption. Further, the maintenance of a suction gas pressure and volume with practically no variation, in place of the 40-60 per cent variation when ambient air is used can result in a compressor life of 20 years instead of, perhaps, 5 years.

Heat collection by ground coil, compared with solar panels, gives approximately 0.551 $kW/h/m^2$ of coil surface for 24 hours per day instead of 0.031 $kW/h/m^2$ of solar panel per 24 hours during each day of the heating season.

# Can I Use My Heat Pump on 'Off peak' Electricity Rates?

For a heat pump with electric motor drive the daily times of operation can affect the price at which electricity may be obtained. Ideally, the heat pump should operate only during the 'off peak' hours during which Electricity Boards supply electricity for domestic purposes at a cheap rate. The advantage to the Electricity Boards of a house heated by an electric motor driven heat pump with a value of C.H. = 3 in place of the use of electric resistance heating is considerable in so far as it reduces demand on generating plant, transformers and cables by two-thirds. The loss to the Boards from existing consumers due to the reduction in the number of units sold, again by two-thirds when a heat pump is used in place of resistance heating, may not be as serious as they anticipate. The several factors now beginning to operate so as to compel large price increases in domestic electricity is likely to influence both existing and potential new customers to change from electric resistance whole house heating to other forms of fuel. There is, however, a large fruitful market awaiting the Electricity Boards in those houses using oil, coal or gas by direct combustion. An electrically driven heat pump with C.H. = 3 would heat these houses more cheaply than by the use of oil, coal or gas. Furthermore, the Electricity Boards have existing sales and other facilities necessary immediately to develop that market.

A heat pump that works only during 'off peak' hours must obviously provide means of heating during peak hours. This can most satisfactorily be done by using underfloor heating, where the heat is stored and gradually released on the same principle as 'storage radiators'. In effect a block of concrete of 400 ft$^3$ or more becomes the low temperature radiator.

An alternative means of storage is to install a much larger hot water tank, in series with the hot water output from the heat pump, than would normally be used for supplying hot water for domestic purposes and to circulate this stored hot water through the radiator, or equivalent, heating system.

If a circulatory warm air system is installed, a hot water storage tank as referred to above can be used, with arrangements for passing the circulated air through or around the tank. Otherwise a warm air circulating system is unlikely to be satisfactory if used during 'off peak' hours only.

# How Would You Design an Efficient Heat Pump?

There are more than one and a half million domestic heat pumps in use in the USA with annual sales of 200,000. Despite the undeniable fuel conservation features which the heat pump offers there is still little demand in Britain and there are probably less than 100 in use. Increases in the price of fuels have recently stimulated home demand.

At the present time no efficient heat pumps for domestic purposes are being made or marketed in Britain. Air-to-air heat pumps of unsatisfactory design are being imported from the USA but it is reported that the averaged ratio of heat output to power input is only 2 to 1. Such a low return makes it difficult to justify the operation of a heat pump driven by an electric motor. I feel justified, having used a semi-sophisticated heat pump for many years with a value of C.H. $= 2.9$, in stating that a specification for a heat pump with a minimum value of C.H. $= 3$ can and should be achieved cheaply and simply.

Consider what this value of C.H. (Practical) of 2 only means when a heat pump is driven by an electric motor, or an oil engine, respectively. For each 1 lb of fuel containing 18,000 Btu (5.28 kW) burned at a modern power station approximately 62 per cent will be wasted, giving 6840 Btu (2kW) as electric power. Transmission and distribution losses will further reduce this amount to about 6000 Btu (1.76 kW) at your electric motor. A value of C.H. = 2 means that the heat pump output to your house is equal to 2 x 6000 or 12,000 Btu (3.52 kW). This is being obtained for 18,000 Btu (5.28 kW) consumed at the power station which is little better in overall fuel economy than an oil fired burner. A value of C.H. = 3 means that 3 x 6000 or 18,000 Btu (5.28 kW) is entering the house, which is equal to the original heat value of the 1 lb of fuel at the power station. No other method of providing heat can give back 100 per cent of the heat originally in the fuel.

Given that a large demand for heat pumps is imminent, there should be established quickly a specification by which several heat pump manufacturers likely to come into the market soon, could test and measure their products and by which purchasers could be reasonably ensured of satisfaction. The following basic data should be supplied with every heat pump:

1.  Guaranteed heat input to house at each of a given range of specified condenser saturation temperatures.
2.  Guaranteed statement of power input to driving motor and auxiliary heater, if any, at each temperature given above.
3.  Guaranteed heat output of the evaporator at specified suction temperatures.

4. Guaranteed statement of Co-efficient of Heating (C.H.), i.e. ratio of Item 1 to Item 2 above with a seasonal minimum of 3.

Technical data and performance as indicated above are made available for motor cars and should therefore be available for heat pumps, which consist of a collection of similar components. Experience in the USA has recently led Electricity Supply Authorities there to take steps to establish standards of performance of heat pumps driven by electric motors because of the high percentage of motor faults and plant failure that are being encountered. These steps are being taken thirty years after sales commenced in the USA. Unless there are presently agreed standards and specifications made now in Britain the problem now about to be met in the USA will occur in this country in about 2000 A.D. In the meantime, anyone proposing to purchase a heat pump would be wise to request and insist upon receiving an answer to each of the four items above. It is suggested also that the value given for the fourth item should be a minimum of 3. If the heat pump was designed correctly this should be possible.

There are, as yet, no signs of any real attention being given in Britain to the design and manufacture of heat pumps. The arbitrary minimum value of C.H. = 3 for an electric motor driven heat pump or C.H. = 4 for an oil driven machine could be improved by attention to design. For example, a compressor and/or a heat engine working on the Stirling Cycle would probably increase these values by a factor of 1.21. Attention which is currently being given to the most suitable future channels of capital investment could well consider directing such investment into University and manufacturing studies of low-grade heat collection and improvement of the direct and reversed heat engine cycle.

# What Should a Heat Pump Cost?

The qualitative answer is to ask what you are likely to save by investing money in a heat pump instead of a direct combustion plant, and what size heat pump you will require. The capital cost should be of the order of 5 per cent of the house value, a point which will be related to a house with a 1500 sq ft floor area, which might cost £25,000. This heat pump will provide 45,000 Btu/h (13.2 kW/h) when the ambient air temperature is 0°C.

At present fuel prices it has been estimated and proved by my own experiment that such a heat pump will save you approximately £750 per year and will have a life of at least 15 years, with an annual maintenance cost which should not exceed £60. You should therefore save £11,250 in 15 years, based on current fuel prices. You may also avoid an expenditure of £500 (equal to a further annual saving of £33) on direct fuel burning plant. If there were further increases in fuel prices your savings would be proportionally increased. Incidentally, you will also have extended the life of non-renewable fossil fuels as well. You will, of course, have lost the interest on about two-thirds of the capital amount invested, but you will still have an investment of about £1500 capable of giving you an annual saving of £750 at 1980 fuel prices.

It is possible to apply the principle of cost-effectiveness to a heat pump installation. Taking a life of 15 years for a heat pump costing £1500 and with a value of C.H. = 3. This machine will reduce the annual cost of electricity by a factor of three, or from £1100 to £366, thus saving £734 per year. On the assumption of future annual increases of 10 per cent in the cost of electricity (a very low assumption), the present cost of £1100 will have risen to £4595 in 15 years. Of this amount the heat pump will save two-thirds with annual maintenance costs no greater than with comparable direct fuel burning plant. Against this annual saving must be set the annual value over 15 years of £1500.

**Table 5**

**Annual fuel saving when using a heat pump to provide 1230 therms per year to a house with a floor area of 1500 sq ft.**

| Heating Method | Fuel and Power used p.a. | | Fuel and Power saved p.a. | |
|---|---|---|---|---|
| | lbs | kW | lbs | kW |
| Direct electric | 31,000 (coal) | 13.5 | – | – |
| Oil firing | 14,000 (oil) | – | – | – |
| Electrical Driven Heat Pump (C.H. = 3) | 10,300 (coal) | 4.5 | 20,700 (coal) | 9.0 |
| Oil Engine Driven Heat Pump (C.H. = 4) | 3500 (oil) | 4.5 | 10,500 (oil) | 9.0 |

The provision of one million heat pumps to replace direct electric heating would reduce coal and electricity consumption at power stations by 10 million tons of coal and give a peak demand of 4500 MW instead of 13,500 MW (allowing no diversity). Assuming that it was desirable, for financial reasons, to replace the diminished loading and consumption which would result, 2 million heat pumps supplied to consumers using oil firing would be necessary thus giving a further saving in oil consumption of 9 million tons. The saving of 25 million tons of coal equivalent per year thus achieved would then have to be equated to the inevitably growing amount of surplus automobile plant and non-productive labour which would be capable of producing 3 million heat pumps. The materials and fully productive labour required to build a mass produced domestic heat pump are of the order of 25 per cent of those required to build a motor car. Since a heat pump can restore as much fuel as is wasted in a motor car the discussion changes from one of 'cost' to the 'value' of a heat pump.

# What Guarantees Can I Expect?

Two major guarantees should be sought, relating to the operation life and performance of a heat pump. Here again, reference will be made to my experience over 15 years with one heat pump used continuously to heat my house. The maintenance carried out over that period has consisted of the replacement of one leaf valve and one topping up with oil, plus an annual checkover taking two hours. This would suggest that a supplier should give a warranty against failure or replacement at least equal to that given by manufacturers of the components.

Guarantees of the performance should commence with the production of a test certificate for each machine giving certified results taken on a fully metered test bed. This would show the certified output of heat per hour and the work input to the driving engine at specified minimum condenser and minimum evaporator temperatures. This certified value of output of heat over work input gives the value of C.H., which would, it is suggested have a minimum value of 3. Either the purchaser and/or the customer must ensure that the source of low-grade heat at the site where the machine will be used is adequate for the demand and will continuously maintain the designed suction pressure over the whole heating season.

# What Life Can I Expect of my Heat Pump?

This is a question that applies to all rotating machinery whether it be a motor car or a heat pump. As with a car a heat pump compressor will last longer if it is not subjected to serious load variations. To maintain constancy of load the temperature of the low-grade heat source should remain as constant as possible. This desideratum can be achieved if a stream, large body of water or a ground coil is used when an annual seasonal temperature variation (and therefore suction pressure) can be kept to within 2 per cent. With air as the low-grade heat source, using a simple circuit as shown in Fig. 3 suction pressure is likely to vary as much as 70 per cent and the pumping capacity by the same amount. Using a ground coil my compressor has run for approximately 45,000 hours over 15 years without appreciable repair or maintenance. With the unsophisticated air-to-air heat pump referred to above the expected life would be considerably reduced, probably to about 5 years, and possibly with a fair amount of maintenance attendance.

If, however, the claims made for the Constempair heat pump as to the provision of a near constant air temperature supply to the evaporator are substantiated, compressor life can be considered on the minimum 15 year basis referred to for the ground coil and water evaporators.

Where ground water from boreholes is used as the low-grade heat source, the water should not be fed directly into the standard double circuit contra-flow evaporator using a number of small bore tubes. Small particles of chalk or grit will collect to restrict water circulation and thus cause freezing up. It is better to feed the water into a small tank into which a small coil is placed through which the refrigerant can circulate.

A well designed electric motor driven domestic heat pump is, of course, equivalent to a larger sized domestic refrigerator but running under more constant load conditions. An annual quick service check is advisable with examination triennially of the house heating system to which the heat pump is attached. Under such conditions the 15 year life already accomplished by my own machine should be applicable to any other properly designed installation.

# Central Heating by the Heat Pump

The central heating of houses in Britain first commenced 1500 years ago when the Romans heated their floors and walls from a hypocaust. The practice fell into disuse until about the beginning of the 19th century when the economy and comfort of central heating was once more recognised. The medium used to heat the room may be air, water or steam. The decision as to the most suitable temperature to maintain in a room is fraught with difficulty.

The use of warmed air as the heating medium is common to most houses in the USA but has found little favour in Britain and Western Europe, where the choice lies between using hot water as the heating medium with standing radiators or pipes laid in the floor, and sometimes the walls and ceilings. The use of standing radiators dates approximately from the beginning of the century and the use of floor, wall and ceiling panels from about 1930.

The use of standing radiators involves isolated units of surface at relatively high temperatures. The remaining surfaces of

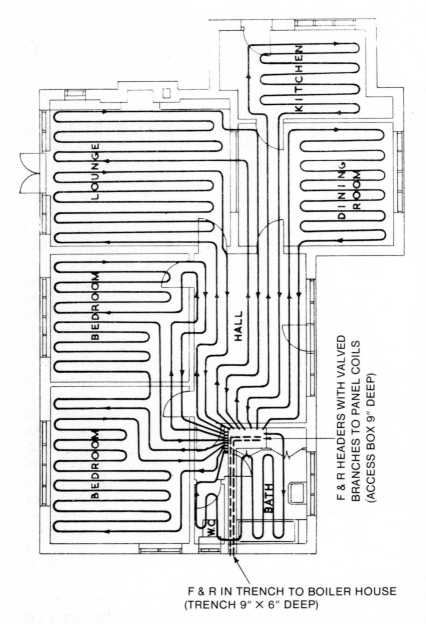

F & R HEADERS WITH VALVED
BRANCHES TO PANEL COILS
(ACCESS BOX 9" DEEP)

F & R IN TRENCH TO BOILER HOUSE
(TRENCH 9" × 6" DEEP)

**Figure 4. Plan of a bungalow showing pipe section layout.**

floor, walls and ceiling remain at much lower temperatures which tend to produce shock because of the considerable temperature differences in various parts of the room.

The installation of pipes conveying hot water in the floor and/or walls is particularly suitable when a heat pump is used. Much of the prejudice against floor heating is due to bad design layout and, particularly, the raising of the floor temperature surfaces to an unacceptably high level. A floor surface temperature should never be allowed to exceed a maximum of 83°F. Yet, in certain cases, I have experienced floor surfaces at 95°F. This means that the temperature of the hot water entering the pipes should not exceed 125°F. Subject to these precautions the use of warmed floors provides the most comfortable and economical method of room heating. For 'off-peak' running of the heat pump there is sufficient reserve of heat in the floor block to carry over the 'off-peak' periods. With a system of heating from warmed surfaces heating of the occupants of the room is by radiation, similar to heating by sunlight. The use of a thermometer as a criterion is therefore of less value than with other systems of heating.

# Can I Use a Heat Pump with my Existing Heating System?

Yes, if you are at present using a hot-air system or a floor wall or ceiling heating system which has hot water circulation. If your house is heated by radiators, which are designed for maximum output with hot water entering at about 160°F (71°C), you may not have sufficient radiator surface to permit a heat pump to keep the house fully heated when ambient air temperatures fall below about 40°F (4.4°C). This is because the normal, single compressor heat pump supplies hot water at a maximum temperature of about 140°F (60°C). But, for probably three quarters of the heating season, or more, the normal heat pump will give sufficient heat output at 125°F to 140°F to heat your house with any well designed existing radiator systems.

As was shown earlier, the estimated maximum heat requirement of 45,000 Btu/h assumed that the air surrounding the house was at 0°C and the inside air at 21°C. An atmospheric air temperature which does not fall below 4.4°C persists for about 90 per cent of the heating season and during this period a heating demand of only about 70 per cent of the 45,000 Btu/h is required. Therefore, the normal heat pump system should supply your radiator system adequately for about 90 per cent of the heating season.

One alternative, if a heat pump is used, is to add one additional radiator for every three or four existing ones and thereby meet all winter heating requirements from the 120-140°F water output.

A second alternative is to install a heat pump which operates in two stages instead of one single stage. A two-stage heat pump is more complicated, but more efficient, than a single-stage machine and can provide hot water at temperatures of 180°F.

# Useful Addresses

Many of the companies listed below manufacture, or are agents for, large scale heat
pumps used in commercial or industrial
applications rather than domestic size
machines. A high proportion of the air-to-air
machines are designed primarily for air conditioning and not as heat pumps, therefore in
any enquiries that you make of the companies
ensure that the heat input and the heat
output specifications are satisfactory when
the machines are put into a heating, rather
than a cooling, mode. Furthermore with this
type of heat pump (air-to-air) bear in mind the
stresses placed on the compressor due to
the highly variable ambient air temperature.
    At the time of writing rumours abound
about major industrial concerns actively
preparing small domestic heat pumps for
launching in the near future. In the absence
of firm knowledge of any of these machines it
is impossible to talk about, or even list, the
manufacturers. Suffice to say that any infor-
mation not included in the listing below
would be appreciated and should be sent to
Prism Press for inclusion in future editions.

| | |
|---|---|
| AAF Ltd<br>Bassington Industrial Estate<br>Cramlington<br>Northumberland NE23 8AF | Water-to-air |
| Aero-Plast<br>Azay-le-Brule<br>79400 Saint-Maizent-L'Ecole<br>France | Air-to-air |
| Airwell<br>78400 Chatou<br>France | Air-to-water/air |
| American Air Filter Co. Inc.<br>215 Central Avenue<br>Louisville<br>Kentucky 40201<br>USA | Water-to-air |
| Anglo Nordic Ltd<br>74 London Road<br>Kingston-upon-Thames<br>Surrey | Air/water-to-water |
| Borg-Warner Ltd<br>715 North Circular Road<br>London NW2 7AU | Air-to-air |
| Robert Bosch GmbH<br>Geschäftsbereich Junkers<br>D7314 Wernau<br>West Germany | Water-to-water |
| Carlyle Air Conditioning Co. Ltd<br>Clifton House<br>Uxbridge Road<br>London W5 5SX | Air-to-air |
| Carrier International Corporation<br>Carrier Parkway<br>Syracuse<br>NY 13201<br>USA | Water/air-to-air |
| Climate Equipment Ltd<br>18 Central Chambers<br>The Broadway<br>Ealing<br>London W5 2NR | Air-to-water<br>(Agents for Hitachi) |

Cliref
Z.L. 'Les Meurieres'
69780 Mions                          Water-to-air/water
France

Command-Aire Corp.
3221 Speight Avenue
Box 7916
Waco
Texas                                Water-to-air
USA

Cool Heat Environment Control
176 High Road                        Air-to-air
London N2 9AS

Corbridge Services
Post Office Buildings
Hill Street
Corbridge on Tyne                    Air/water-to-water
Northumberland NE45 5AA

CTC Heat
296b Station Road
Harrow                               Ground-to-water/air
Middlesex

Dunham-Bush International
175 South Street
West Hartford
Connecticut 06110                    Water-to-water
USA

Dunham-Bush Ltd
Fitzherbert Road
Farlington                  Water-to-water (large scale)
Portsmouth PO6 1RR

EER Air Conditioning Products Ltd
Brittania House
Ashton-under-Lyme                    Air-to-air
Lancs OL7 0PP

Enviro-Aesthetic Engineering
9 Albion Place
Maidstone                            Air-to-air
Kent ME14 5DY

FGF Equipment
62 Rue du Faubourg Poissonnière
75010 Paris                     Air-to-air/water
France

Fläkt (UK) Ltd
Staines House
158 High Street
Staines                         Air-to-air
Middlesex TW18 4AR

AB Svenska Fläktfabriken
Fack
104 60 Stockholm               Air-to-air (large scale)
Sweden

Friedrich Air Conditioning and Refrigeration Co.
4200 North PanAm Expressway
PO Box 1540
San Antonio
Texas 78295                     Air/water-to-air
USA

General Electric Co.
Central Air Conditioning Dept
Appliance Park Building 6
Louisville
Kentucky 40225                  Air-to-air
USA

Girdwood Halton (Air Conditioning) Ltd
18-20 Thorpe Road
Norwich                         Water-to-air
Norfolk NR1 1RY

Grenco Bedrijfskoeling BV
Postbus 205
S'Hertogenbosch        Ground/air/water-to-air/water
Holland

Heat-Frig Ltd
Torrie Lodge
Portsmouth Road
Esher                  Air-to-air, water-to-water
Surrey

Hitachi Ltd
6-2 2-Chome
Otemachi
Chiyoda-ku
Tokyo                              Air-to-water
Japan

Hitachi Zosen
Hitachi Shipbuilding & Engineering Co. Ltd
6-14 Edobori
1-Chome, Nishi-Ku
Osaka 550                          Air-to-air
Japan

Hitachi Zosen International SA
Winchester House
77 London Wall                     Air-to-air
London EC2N 1BQ

Lennox Industries Ltd
P.O. Box 43
Lister Road
Basingstoke                        Air-to-air
Hants

Metro
Bymosevej 1-3
DK-3200 Helsinge           Air/water-to-water
Denmark

ML Refrigeration and Air Conditioning Ltd
292 Leigh Road
Trading Estate
Slough                     (Agents for Fedders (USA))
Bucks

Natural Energy Centre
2 York Street                Air-to-water (also offer
London W1          consulting and advisory services)

Northern Engineering Industries Ltd
P.O. Box 1NT
Cuthbert House
All Saints
Newcastle on Tyne          (Agent for Westinghouse)
NE99 1NT

Sinclaire Air Conditioning Ltd
22 Queen Anne's Gate
Westminster                           Air-to-air (Agents for
London SW1H 9AH                          General Electric)

Singer Co.
Climate Control Division
1300 Federal Boulevard
Carteret New Jersey 07008                  Water-to-air
USA

Sulzer Bros (UK) Ltd
Farnborough
Hampshire

Sulzer Bros Ltd
CH-8401 Winterthur
Switzerland

Sulzer Bros (South Africa) Ltd
Johannesburg 2000
P.O. Box 930
South Africa

Sulzer-Escher Wyss GmbH
D-8990 Lindau-Bodensee
Postfach 1380              Ground/water/air-to-air/water
West Germany

Technibel SA
Route Départmentale 28
Reyrieux
01600 Trevoux                    Air-to-air (large scale)
France

Temperature Ltd
192-206 York Road                        Water-to-air
London SW11 3SS

Trane
Commercial Air Conditioning Division
La Crosse
WI 54601              Water-to-air/water (large scale)
USA

Ventiheat ApS
Mollegade
DK-6640 Lunderskov                       Air-to-water
Denmark

Vestfrost
Spansbjerg Mollevej 100
DK-6700 Esbjerg                        Air-to-water
Denmark

A S Volund
Varmeterknisk Sektor
Prindalsvej 1
DK-6920 Videbaek                    Ground-to-water
Denmark

Walker Air Conditioning Ltd
136 Strathmore Road
Balmore Industrial Estate          (agents  for  Carlyle)
Glasgow G22 7TA

Weathermaker Equipment Ltd
Churchill House
Talbot Road
Old Trafford              Air-to-air (agents for Carlyle)
Manchester M16 0BA

Weltemp Ltd
6 Ark Road
Kingston upon Thames                   Air-to-air
Surrey KT2 6EF

Westinghouse
Commercial-Industrial
Templifier Department
Staunton                   Water-to-water (large scale)
Virginia 24401

Westinghouse Electric
1 The Curfew Yard
Thames Street
Windsor
Berkshire

Zohar Engineering Co. Ltd
13 Nakhalat-Benjamin Street
65-161 Tel Aviv                        Air-to-air
Israel